History's Mysteries

The Egyptian Pyramids: How Did They Get Built?

MEGAN COOLEY PETERSON

BLACK RABBIT BOOKS

Bolt is published by Black Rabbit Books
P.O. Box 227, Mankato, Minnesota, 56002.
www.blackrabbitbooks.com

Jennifer Besel, editor; Grant Gould, designer;
Omay Ayres, photo researcher

Library of Congress Cataloging-in-Publication Data
Names: Peterson, Megan Cooley, author.
Title: The Egyptian pyramids : how did they get built? / by Megan Cooley Peterson. Description: Mankato, Minnesota : Black Rabbit Books, 2019. | Series: Bolt | Series: History's mysteries | Audience: 008-012. | Audience: 4 to 6.
Identifiers: LCCN 2017039236 (print) | LCCN 2017040866 (ebook) | ISBN 9781680725254 (ebook) | ISBN 9781680724097 (library binding) | ISBN 9781644662564 (paperback)
Subjects: LCSH: Pyramids—Egypt—Juvenile literature.
Classification: LCC DT63 (ebook) | LCC DT63 .P475 2019 (print) | DDC 932/.01—dc23
LC record available at https://lccn.loc.gov/2017039236

Image Credits

Alamy: Dan Breckwoldt, 12; Sophie McAulay, 10–11 (pyramid); Stephan Karg, 22–23 (mummy); Tor Eigeland, 6 (bkgd), 26–27; Bigstock: zanskar, Cover (pyramids); commons.wikimedia.org: F l a n k e r, 16–17; Twthmoses, 24; iStock: Givaga, Cover (back pyramid), 4–5; Hanis, 22 (bkdg); Science Source: New York Public Library, 18; Shutterstock: Canicula, 29 (monuments); dovla982, 6–7 (map); Dudarev Mikhail, 32; Fogen, 11 (block); Fred Mantel, 21; George W. Bailey, 31; Igor Zh., 25 (lightning); Jeremy Red, 1, 25 (pyramid); Maria Isaeva, Cover, 29 (magnifying glass); matrioshka, 3; Oleg Golovnev, 29 (paper); Ralph Hackeland, 8–9 (map); Rashevskyi Viacheslav, 9 (pyramid); veleknez, 13; WitthayaP, 15; Zanna Art, Cover (half circle)

CONTENTS

CHAPTER 1

SECRETS in Stone

Huge pyramids rise from the desert in Egypt. For thousands of years, people have wondered how they were built. And they wonder what secrets hide inside.

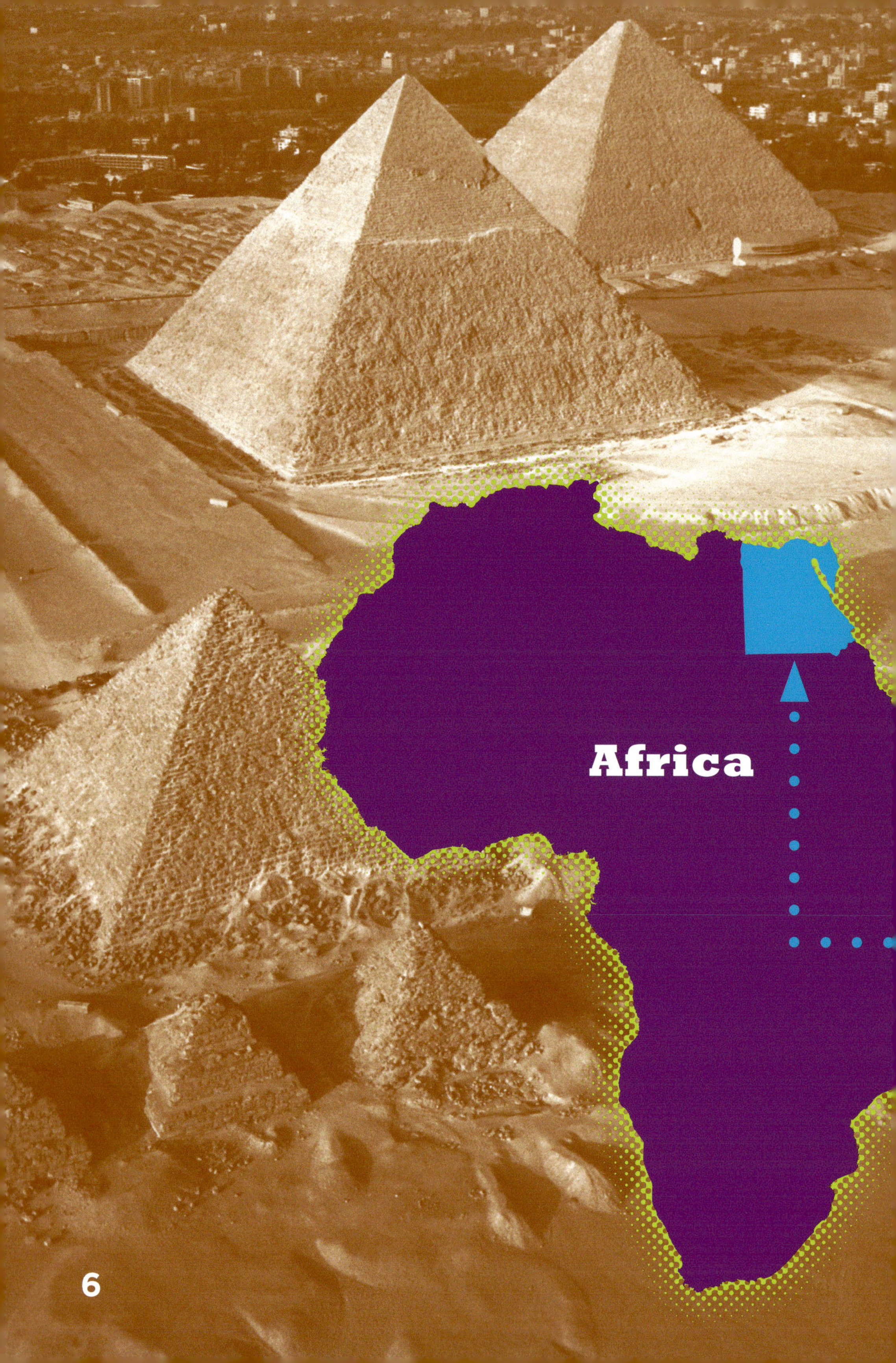
Africa

Very Old Buildings

Egypt is home to more than 100 pyramids. Most historians agree they were built between 2700 and 1700 BC. That's about 4,000 years ago! But people don't agree on how or why they were built.

SOME PYRAMIDS IN EGYPT
Mediterranean Sea
Great Pyramid

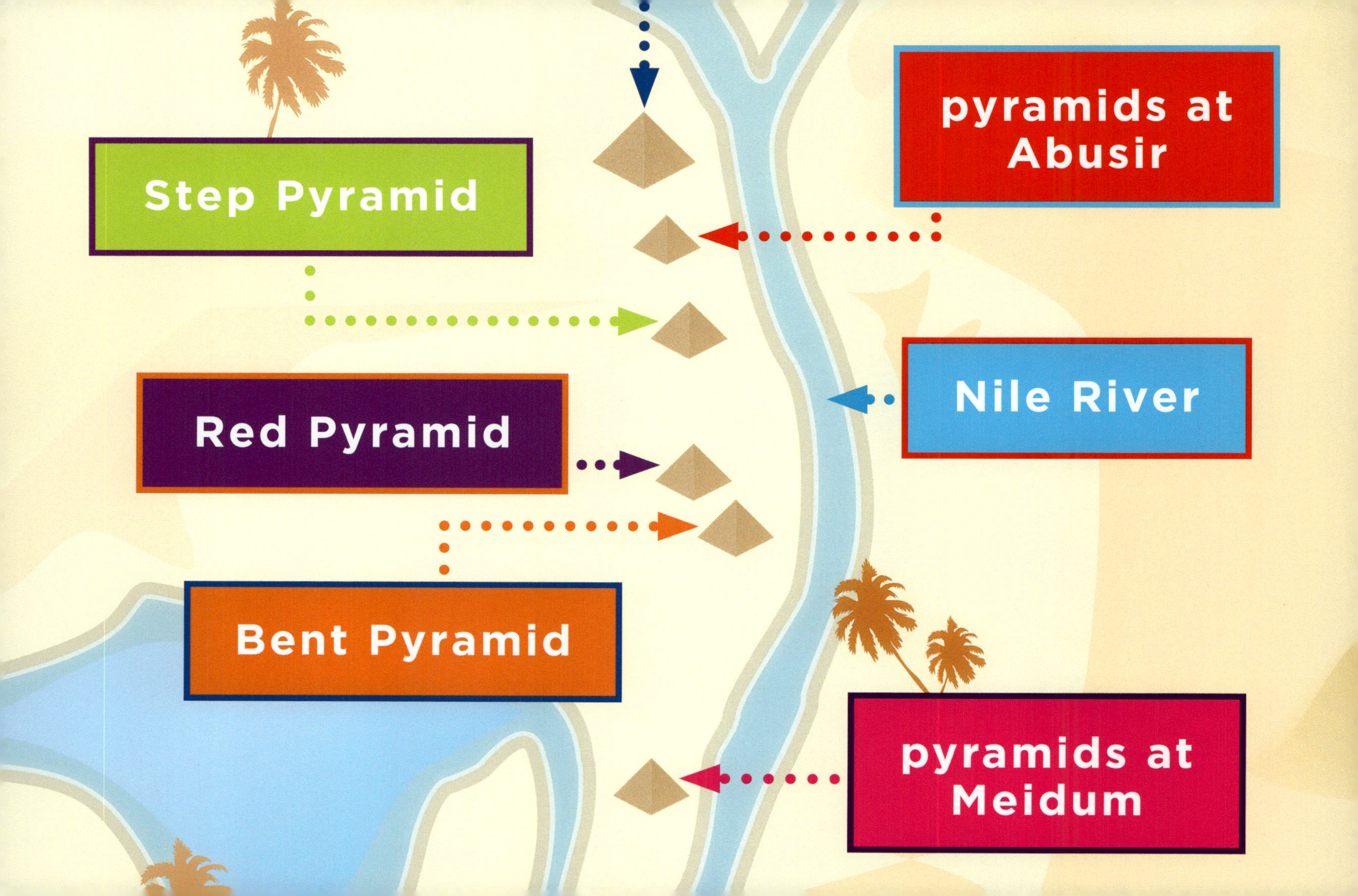
Step Pyramid
pyramids at Abusir
Red Pyramid
Nile River
Bent Pyramid
pyramids at Meidum

CHAPTER 2

INVESTIGATING the Pyramids

The pyramids are huge. Builders used limestone and granite stones. The Great Pyramid alone has more than 2 million blocks. Each block weighs an **average** of 5,000 pounds (2,268 kilograms).

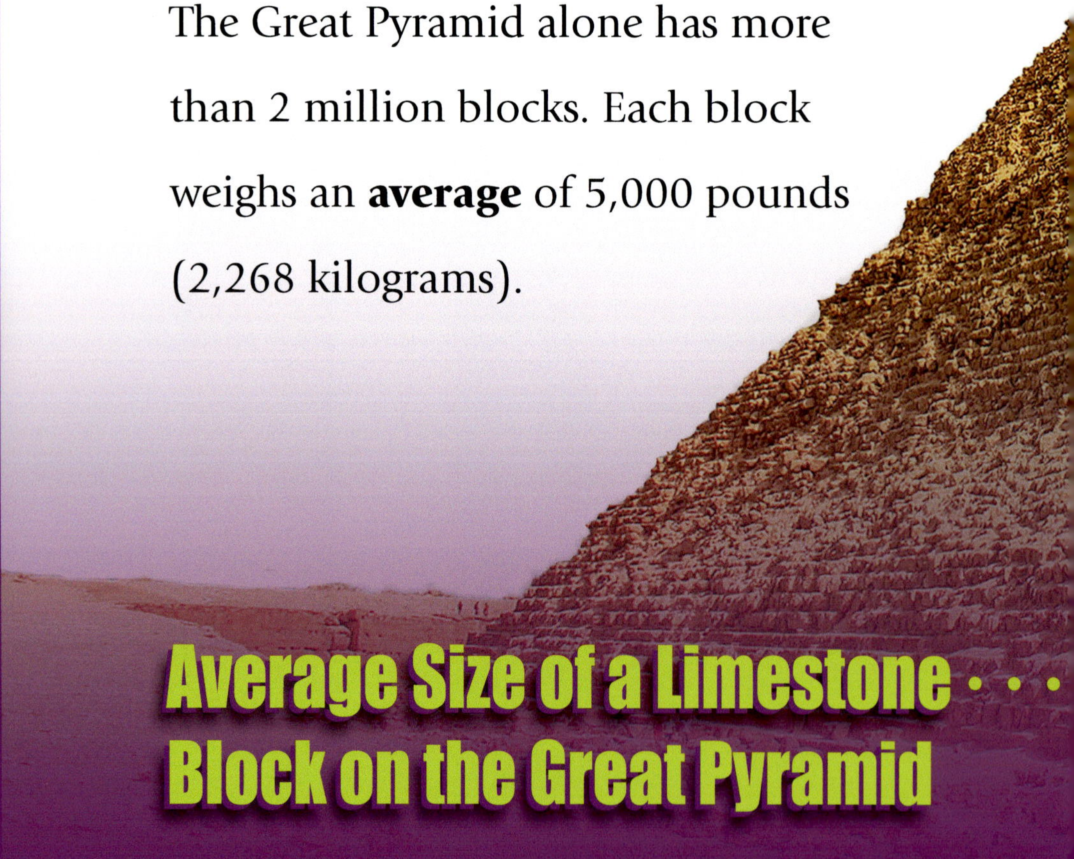

Average Size of a Limestone Block on the Great Pyramid . . .

50 inches
(127 cm)
wide
28 inches
(71 centimeters)
tall
50 inches
(127 cm)
long

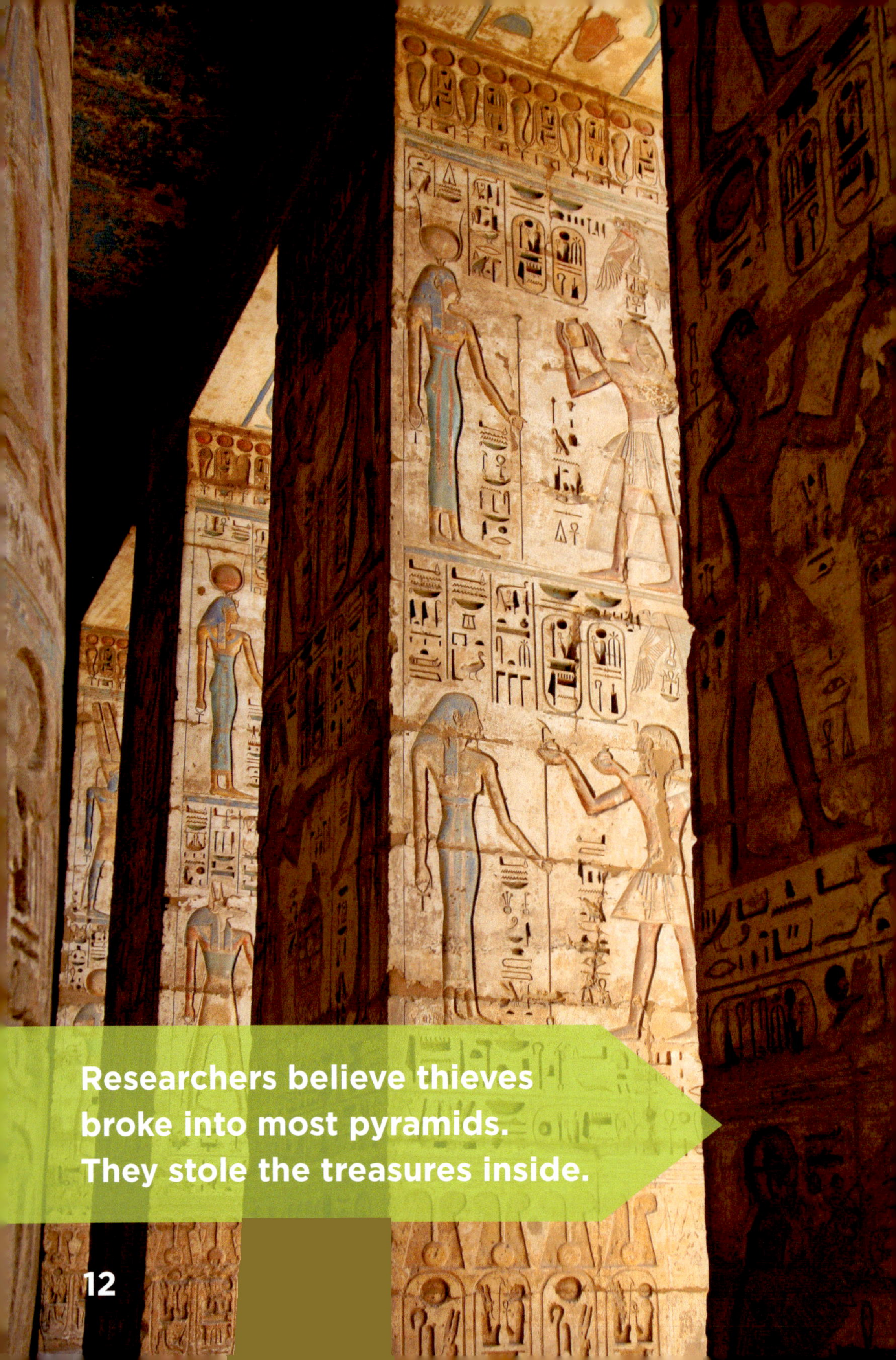

Researchers believe thieves broke into most pyramids. They stole the treasures inside.

Rooms in the Pyramids

Most pyramids have small chambers. Artwork decorates some chamber walls. A room in the Great Pyramid holds an empty **sarcophagus**. Researchers found a mummified foot in one of the Step Pyramid's chambers.

Mysterious Tunnels

The Great Pyramid has four small tunnels. No one knows why workers built them. In 1993, a researcher sent a camera into one of the **shafts**. It sent back a photo. The photo showed a stone blocking the way. Is it a door?

Bent Pyramid
344 feet
(105 m)
Great Pyramid
481 feet
(147 m)

INSIDE THE GREAT PYRAMID

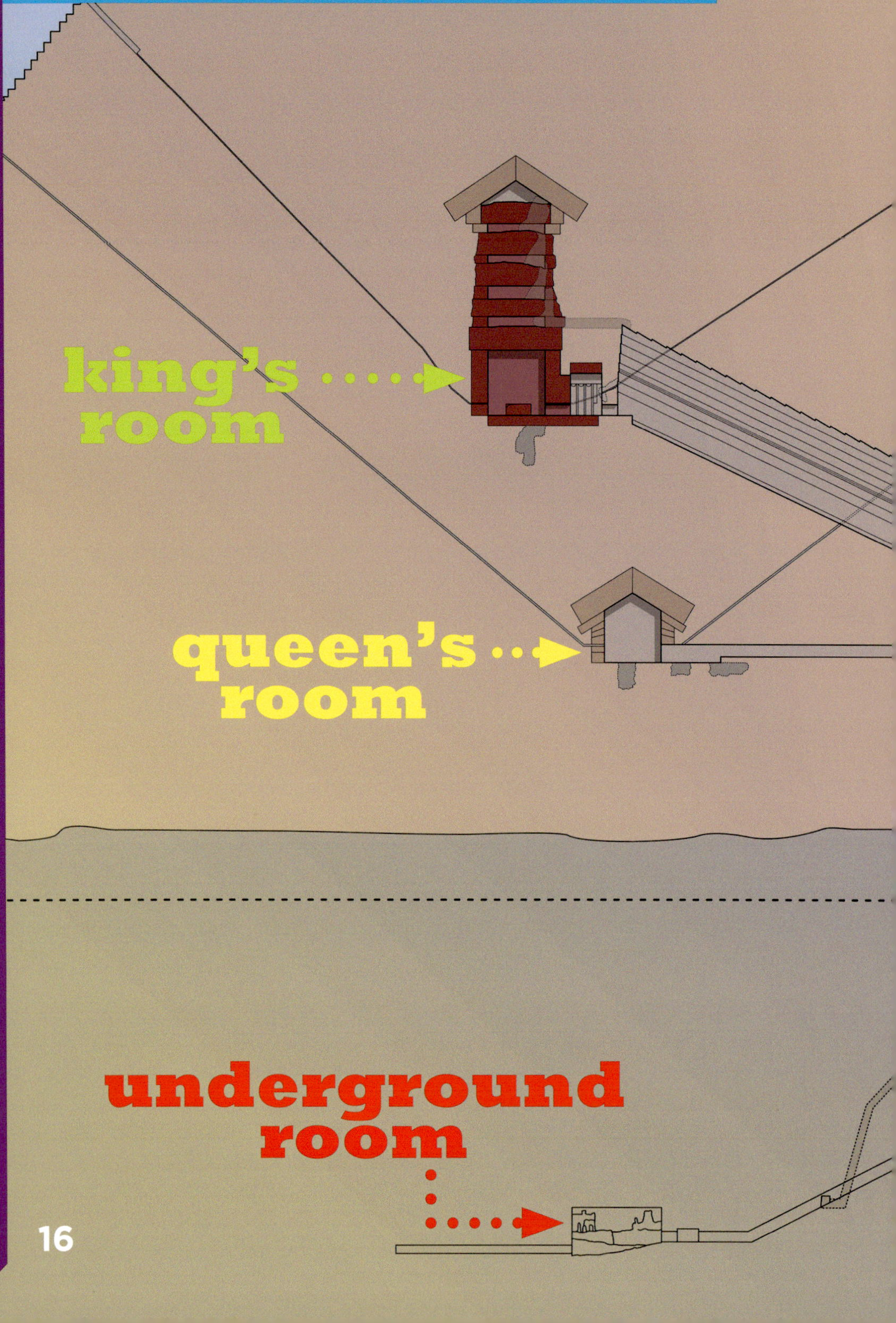

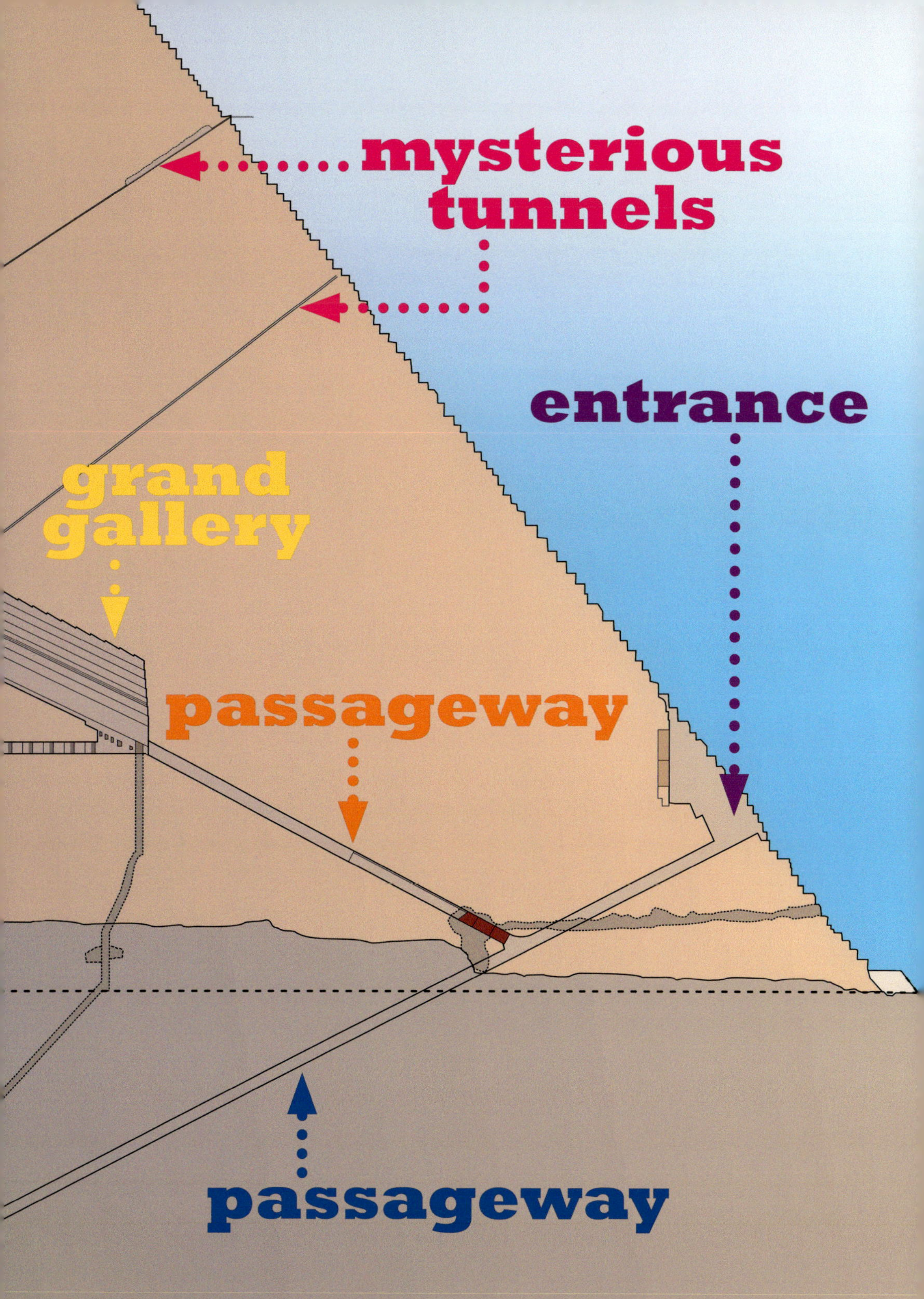
mysterious tunnels
entrance
grand gallery
passageway
passageway

CHAPTER 3

Pyramid THEORIES

Ancient Egyptians did not have **advanced** machines. So how did they build the huge pyramids? Scientists say workers cut stones from **quarries**. They pulled the stones on sleds. They might have also floated them down the Nile River.

At the pyramid, workers had to raise the stones. Researchers have found parts of ramps at some pyramids. Workers might have dragged stones up ramps.

Mind Power

Not everyone believes ancient people could build the pyramids. Some people think Egyptians had something like magic powers. One idea is that they had **devices** with laser beams. The beams could lift stones into the air.

Some people believe aliens built the Egyptian pyramids.

Royal Tombs

Many questions remain about why pyramids were built too. Most researchers believe they are kings' tombs. Workers carved **hieroglyphs** at many pyramid sites. These carvings were to help the kings' souls go to the next life.

A Power Plant?

Not everyone believes pyramids were tombs. Some people claim the Great Pyramid was a power plant. It made energy. They argue that a stone carving shows ancient Egyptians using light bulbs. Did the Great Pyramid power them?

Many Egyptian royals weren't buried in pyramids. The Valley of the Kings is a royal cemetery. Workers carved tombs into rock walls. Could this prove pyramids weren't tombs?

CHAPTER 4

You Decide

The Egyptian pyramids are world famous. They are one of history's great mysteries. Did the pyramids hold Egypt's kings? Did humans or aliens build them? The answers may still lie buried in the sand.

Asking Questions to Solve the Mystery

Researchers ask questions to solve history's mysteries. You can too!

WHO? Who built the pyramids?

WHAT? What rooms might be hidden inside?

WHEN? When did they build the pyramids?

WHERE? Where did the materials and workers come from?

WHY? Why were the pyramids built?

HOW? How were the pyramids built?

What other questions do you have?

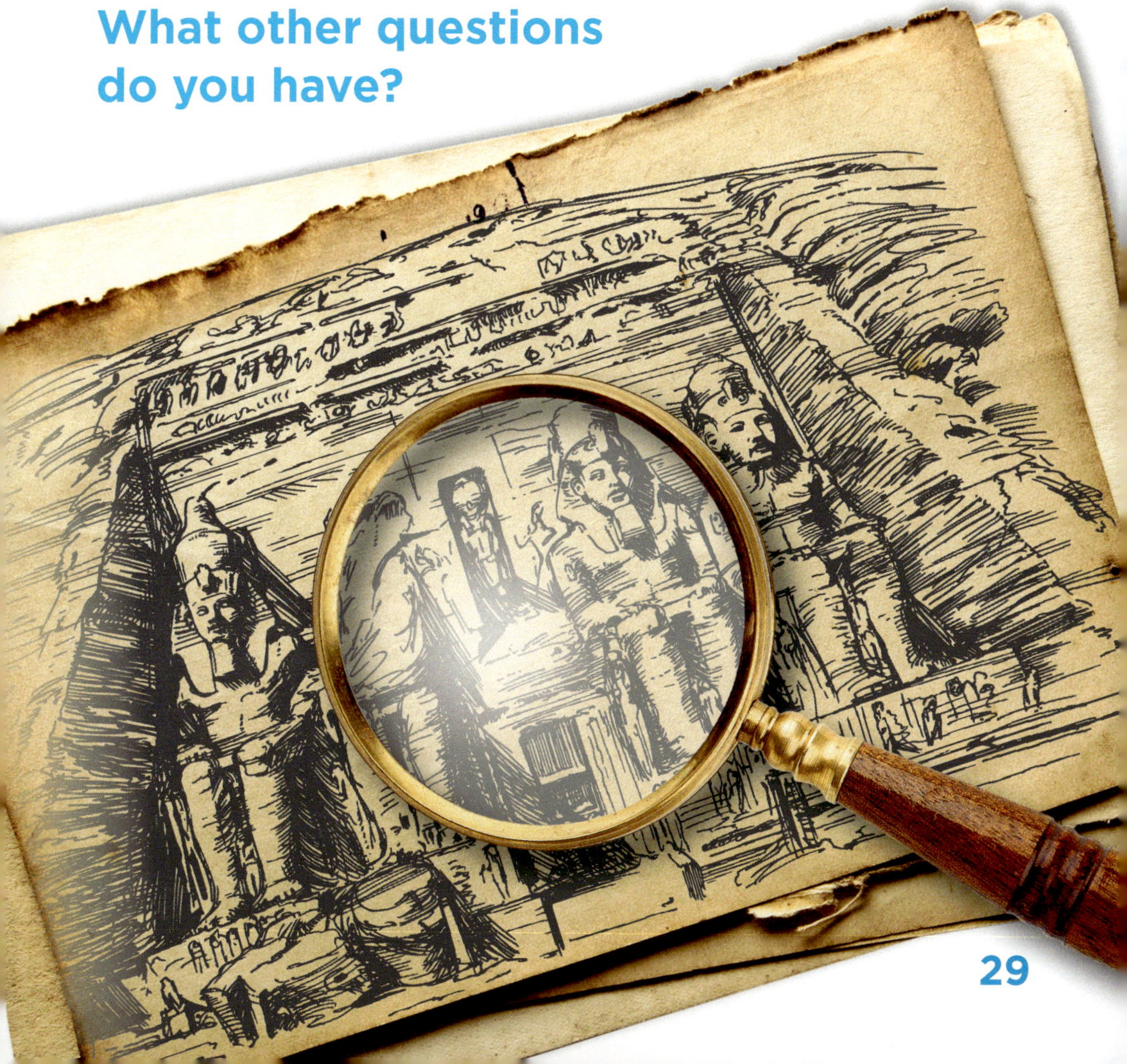

advanced (ad-VANSD)—being beyond others in progress

ancient (AYN-shunt)—from a long time ago

average (AHV-rij)—a number that is calculated by adding quantities together and then dividing the total by the number of quantities

device (dee-VIS)—an object, machine, or piece of equipment made for a special purpose

hieroglyph (HYE-ruh-glif)—a picture or symbol used in the ancient Egyptian system of writing

quarry (KWOR-ee)—a place where stone is dug out of the ground

sarcophagus (sar-KAH-fuh-guhs)—a stone coffin

shaft (SHAFT)—an opening or passage through the floors of a building

LEARN MORE

BOOKS

Kenney, Karen Latchana. *Mysteries of the Egyptian Pyramids.* Ancient Mysteries. Minneapolis: Lerner Publications, 2017.

Marsh, Laura. *Pyramids.* National Geographic Kids Readers. Washington, D.C.: National Geographic, 2017.

McCall, Henrietta. *Pyramid.* Time Shift. Jonesville, MI: Book House, 2015.

WEBSITES

Egyptian Pyramid Facts
www.sciencekids.co.nz/sciencefacts/engineering/egyptianpyramids.html

Memphis and Its Necropolis–The Pyramid Fields from Giza to Dahshur
whc.unesco.org/en/list/86

Seven Wonders of the Ancient World
kids.nationalgeographic.com/explore/history/seven-wonders/#Pyramids-at-Giza.png

INDEX